Lattice smocking

Leona Lehner

δελος

CAPE TOWN

This book would not have been possible without all the ladies in our classes, who gave me their help and encouragement and provided me with exciting new ideas. My grateful thanks also go to Alida Botha for checking the text and the patterns.

Also available in Afrikaans as *Traliesmokwerk*

Translated by Wordwise Language Service
Photography by André Stander
Illustrations by Leona Lehner
Cover design by Richard Jones
Book design by Corrine Lancaster
Set in 10 on 12pt Souvenir Roman
Printed and bound by Associated Printing, Cape Town

First edition 1991

ISBN 1-86826-149-2

Contents

Introduction

I remember once seeing some beautiful plaited, velvet cushions in the home of an elderly couple. Little did I dream then that I would one day be able to make such cushions myself! That was the only lattice smocking I have come across. It is still not well known today and very few articles have appeared in handcraft books.
Lattice smocking is also known as Canadian or North American smocking but whether it really did originate on the North American continent is a moot point – I was unable to find anything about the history of this type of smocking.
I have been giving classes for the past couple of years in gingham smocking; lattice smocking has formed part of these classes.
With time, I have been able to add a number of variations that allow lattice smocking to be used for much more than the traditional velvet cushions. It is particularly effective for modern evening dresses, bridal gowns, tracksuits, cushions and other articles made from satin.
The basic stitch is relatively easy and a piece of fabric can quickly be transformed into a work of art with beautiful plaited patterns.
I hope and trust this book will help to give lattice smocking a new lease of life.

Leona Lehner
Windhoek 1990

Lattice smocking

Lattice smocking cannot really be compared with ordinary smocking; with lattice smocking, fabric is gathered in both directions and it is therefore more closely related to smocking on the straight grain of gingham, which is, at times, referred to as North American smocking. It requires evenly spaced rows of dots to be made on the back of fabric, which is then gathered between various dots to form pleats with a plaited appearance on the front of the fabric. In contrast with ordinary smocking, which is very elastic horizontally, lattice smocking is less elastic but it does stretch both horizontally and vertically.

Lattice smocking can be cut after the smocking has been done without the stitches pulling out. A piece of fabric can therefore first be smocked before a pattern is cut out of it for a garment. This procedure is well suited to, for example, smocked shoulder pieces, sleeves and panels.

Fabric and thread

Lattice smocking is traditionally done on velvet, on which it is, indeed, very effective. It can also be done on cotton velvet, synthetic velvet, fine and soft corduroy, lightweight upholstery fabric, satins, taffeta, certain types of tracksuit fabric, knits and a wide variety of crease-resistant synthetic fabric.

Basic lattice smocking requires double the width and length of the finished piece. Variations with rows left open in between require less fabric. To ensure there will be enough fabric, it may be advisable to cut the fabric only after the smocking has been done. Rows of smocking can then, if necessary, be extended.

The thread used for lattice stitch depends on the thickness and type of fabric that is smocked. Thin pearl cotton thread, thin crochet yarn or a double length of polyester sewing thread is used for satin and other lightweight fabric. Thick pearl cotton thread, thick crochet yarn or a double length of no. 10 sewing thread is used for heavy fabric.

Marking the dots

Evenly spaced rows of dots are marked on the back of the fabric. This is time-consuming but the evenness of the dots determines the neatness of the pleats, so it is well worth the trouble. The width of the pleats is half the distance between the dots. Dots 30 mm apart, for example, form 15 mm pleats. The thicker and heavier the fabric, the wider the pleats should be. For large articles, it is advisable to smock a small sample piece first; this will show whether the width of the pleats is suitable for the type of fabric.

The first row of dots is marked in line either with the selvage or with the grain of the fabric. A fabric thread can be pulled to create a straight line if necessary. The dots are marked in pencil, air or water-soluble ink pen or tailor's-tacks. I have even used a moistened, light-coloured colour pencil on dark fabric with great success. A ruler and triangle are used to ensure the rows are perpendicular. Satin and soft fabric should be stuck with adhesive tape to a table or an even surface to prevent it from shifting while it is being marked. The entire area to be smocked should be marked before smocking is started.

Neatening the smocked work

If stiff satin or taffeta is used, some of the pleats sometimes do not fold neatly on the front of the fabric. Neaten them by inserting the back of a pencil or a thick knitting needle at the back through the pleat. After neatening all the pleats, the piece of work can be pressed slightly by placing a book on top. Do not flatten the pleats by ironing them.

Joining fabric

When a belt or large article is made, the fabric may have to be joined. The nap should run in the same direction on both sides of the join. The dots are marked so that the middle row of dots of a row is on the join. When the pleats are formed, the join will then be almost invisible.

Washing and care

Lattice smocking should be washed very carefully by hand. Velvet articles should be dry-cleaned. The pleats on other fabric should be straightened while still wet; they should never be ironed. Articles made from crease-resistant fabric can simply be washed and hung to dry.

Basic lattice smocking

Basic lattice stitch is worked on the back of the fabric. The pleats on the front of the fabric create the lattice effect. The dots and joining stitches do not show on the front after the pleats have been made.

Fig. A shows the sequence for two rows of basic lattice smocking. Start in the top left corner and smock one row at a time. Figs. B to F show how the rows are smocked. Start at 1, pick up the dots at 2 and 1 and work together with two stitches (Fig. B), making sure not to catch the pleat at the back. Pick up the dot at 3 (Fig. C). Keep the thread between 2 and 3 straight and knot it at 3 by passing it under the previous thread and pulling it down (Fig. D). Join the dots at 4 and 3 with two stitches (Fig. E) and proceed to 5 where the thread should be knotted again (Fig. F). Continue for the full length of the row. To smock the second and subsequent rows, start in the same way as the first. In other words, if the first row was started on the top left dot, all the other rows are also started on the top left dot of a row.

An alternative method

If heavy or thick fabric is smocked, another method can be used to join the dots. Use strong thread and pick up the first two dots, gather the two sides of the fabric tightly together and make a knot by passing the needle under the thread (Fig. G). Proceed to 3 and knot the thread as shown.

Reverse basic lattice smocking

The back of basic lattice smocking is very attractive and can therefore also be used on the front of the piece of work. The dots are then marked on the front of the fabric and the smocking is also worked on the front of the fabric.

To work the first stitch, leave the knot in the thread at the back, bring the needle out at 1 and join 2 and 1 with one stitch (Fig. B). To work the second stitch, push the pleat at the back up with your finger, insert the needle at 2 and bring it out at 3 (Fig. H). Keep the thread between 2 and 3 straight and sew a small backstitch at 3. Join the dots at 4 and 3 and pass the needle at the back to 5. The joining stitches now show on the front of the fabric. If pearl cotton thread or other embroidery yarn is used, the joining stitches can be made to look attractive. A bead or pearl can be sewn on to cover the joining stitches. To do this, join the two dots with one stitch, thread the needle through the bead and work the second stitch.

If stiff satin is used and the pleats do not fold neatly, flatten the pleat at the back as it should fold instead of pushing it upwards. The second joining stitch is then in the centre of the pleat at the back. This is the method followed for the satin waistcoat.

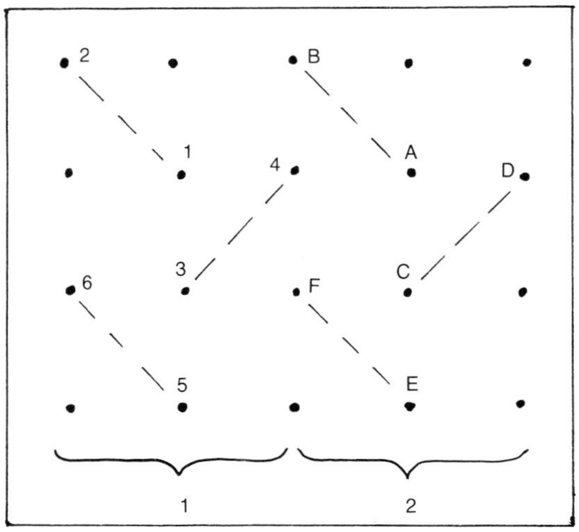

Fig. A

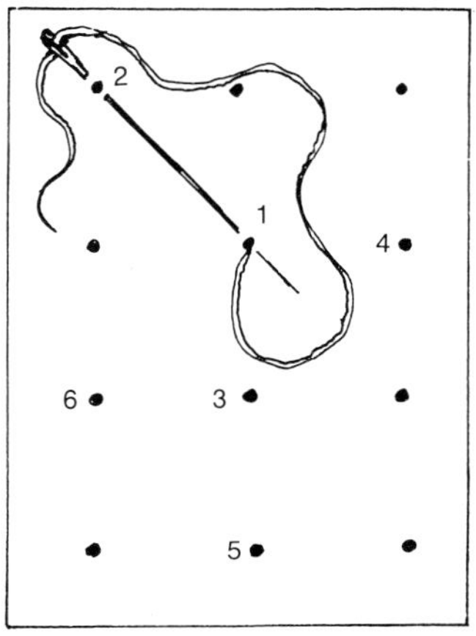

Fig. B

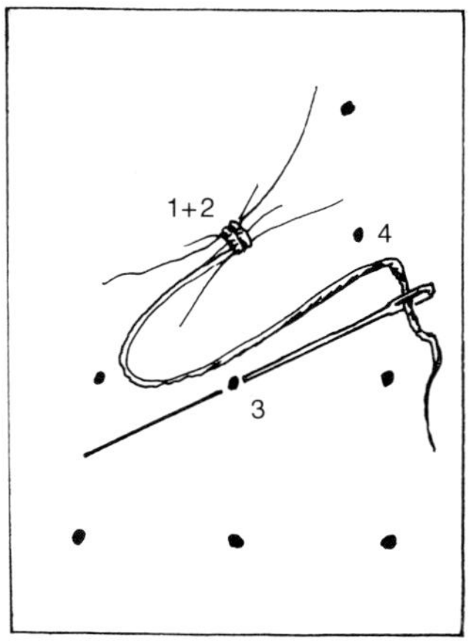

Fig. C

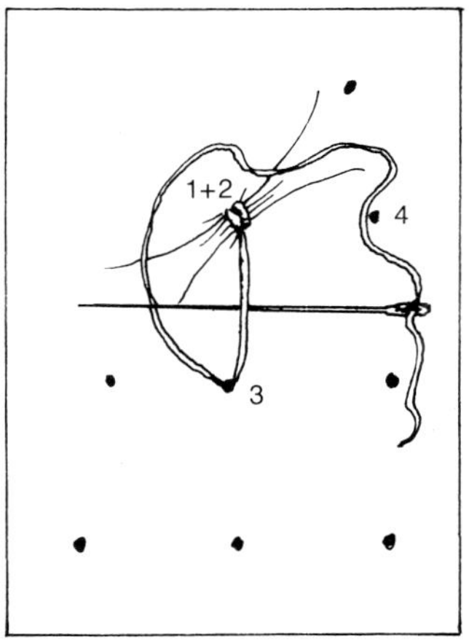

Fig. D

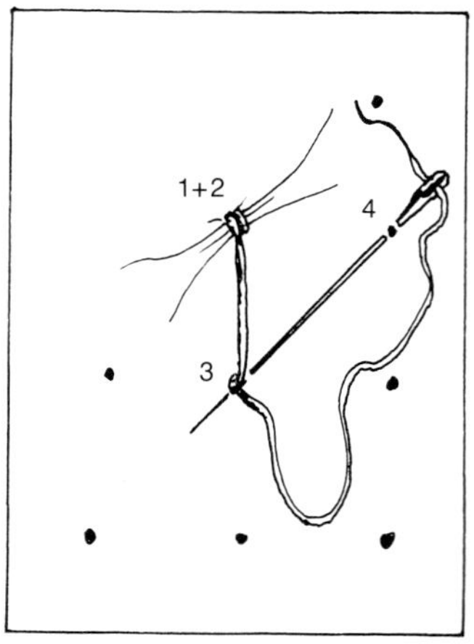

Fig. E

Reverse basic

Basic

Alternate sides

Open rows

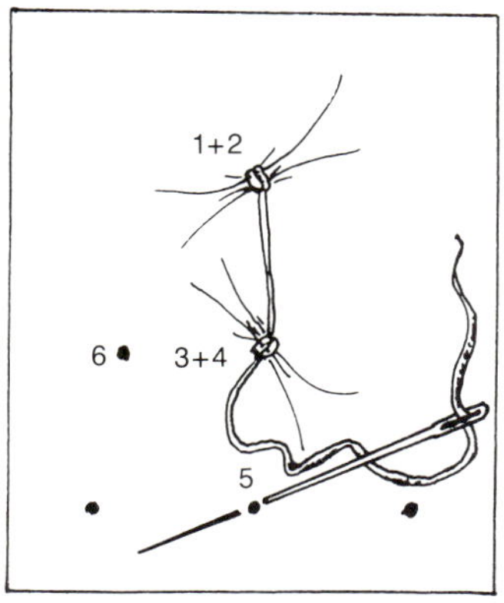

Fig. F

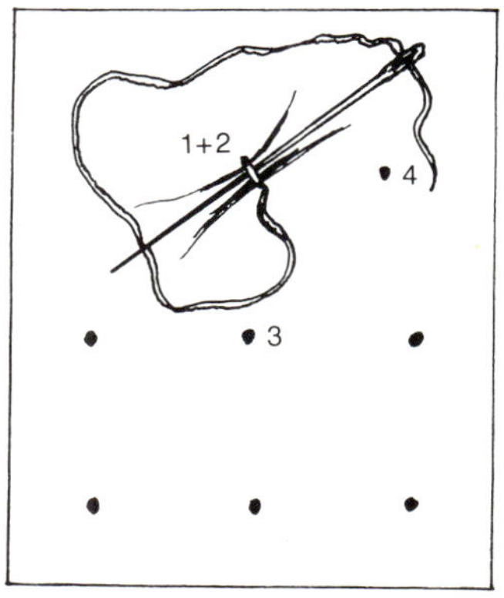

Fig. G

Leaving open rows in between

Beautiful variations can be obtained with lattice smocking if half or full rows are left open. When the back of the fabric is smocked, all the rows can be marked and the dots of the row left open can then simply be skipped. When the front is worked, only the dots to be worked are marked. The dots to be skipped can, however, be marked with air-soluble ink. Care should be taken if water-soluble ink is used on satin or taffeta – the water can leave marks.

Fig. I shows how two rows of dots with half a row left open are marked. Fig. J shows two rows with one row left open and Fig. K shows one and a half rows left open.

Rows on alternate sides

Further variations can be obtained if some rows are smocked on the front of the fabric and some on the back. The rows are marked alternately on the front and back of the fabric, unless the fabric is transparent, in which case they can be marked on the back of the fabric.

Fig. L shows how these rows are marked. Rows 1 and 3 are marked and smocked on the back of the fabric. Row 2 is marked on the front and smocked in the opposite direction. The spaces between the rows can be enlarged to vary the pleats and to suit the type of fabric.

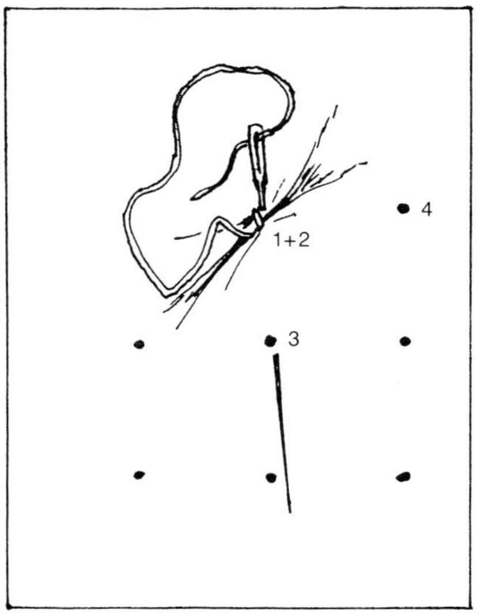

Fig. H

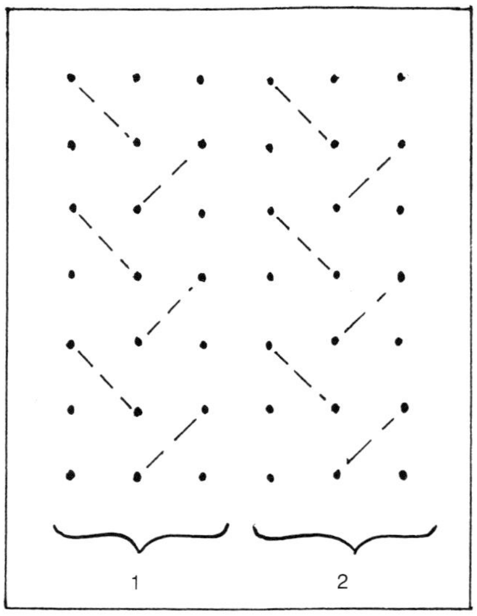

Fig. I

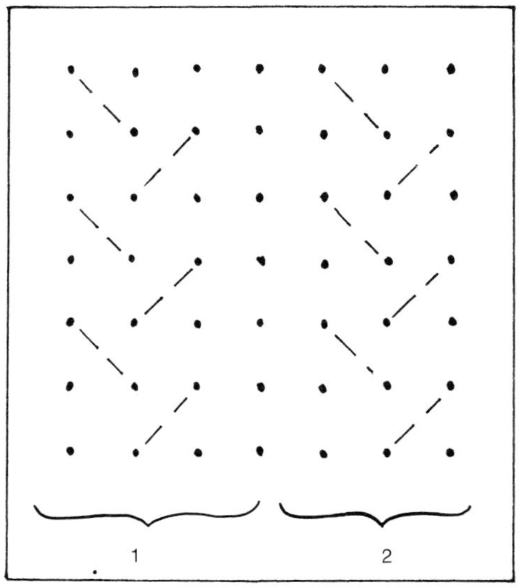

Fig. J

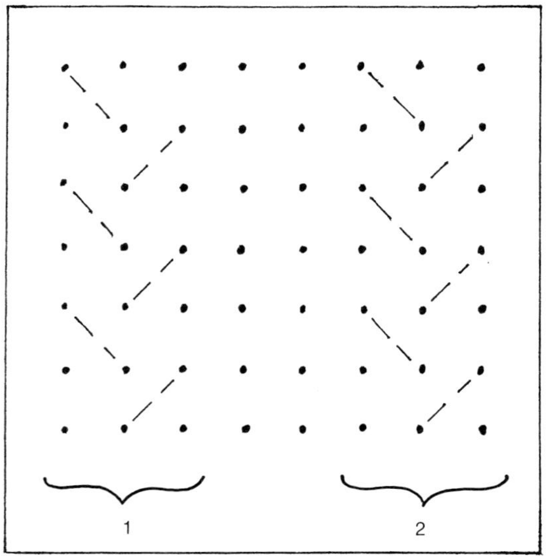

Fig. K

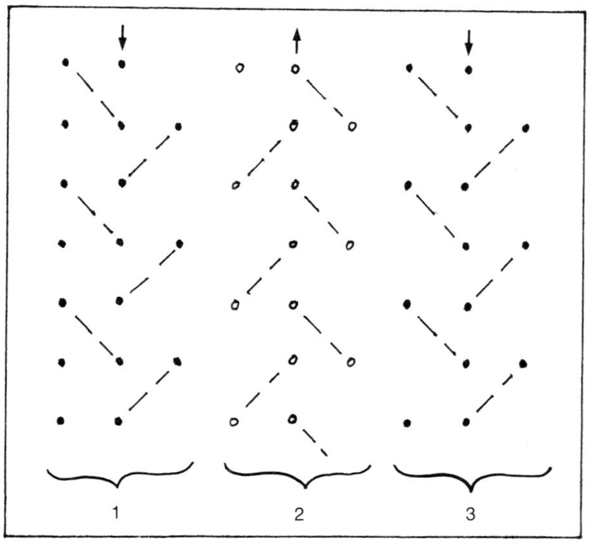

Fig. L

Square velvet cushion

This cushion measures 38 cm x 38 cm. Only the front of the cushion was smocked. A couple of these cushions can be made in colours to match a lounge suite.

MATERIALS

150 cm cotton or other velvet, 90 cm wide
Strong matching sewing thread
38 cm zip
36 cm x 36 cm cushion

METHOD

Cut a 90 cm x 90 cm piece of fabric for the front of the cover. Mark 30 mm spaced dots on the back. Make sure the first row is in line with the selvage. Mark 27 dots in the first row and 26 rows of dots. Follow the method for basic lattice stitch and smock 13 rows.

Cut a 42 cm x 42 cm piece of fabric for the back of the cover. Neatly fold the pleats around the edges of the smocked front and pin or tack (Fig. 1). Stitch the zip to one side of the smocked front (F) and one side of the back (B) of the cover (Fig. 2). Fold the fabric in half at the zip with the right sides together and, making sure the finished cover will measure 38 cm x 38 cm, stitch the other three seams 20 mm from the edge (Fig. 3).

Cut the seam edges even if necessary and finish off, using overcast or zigzag stitches. Turn the right side out through the zip opening. Lightly press the seams if necessary. Insert the cushion and there you have it – a work of art and an heirloom!

Variations: Both sides of the cushion-cover can be smocked, using 180 cm x 90 cm fabric. Piping can be added to the edges. The zip can be inserted in the centre of the back. Satin can be used and a frill can be added to the edges.

Fig. 1

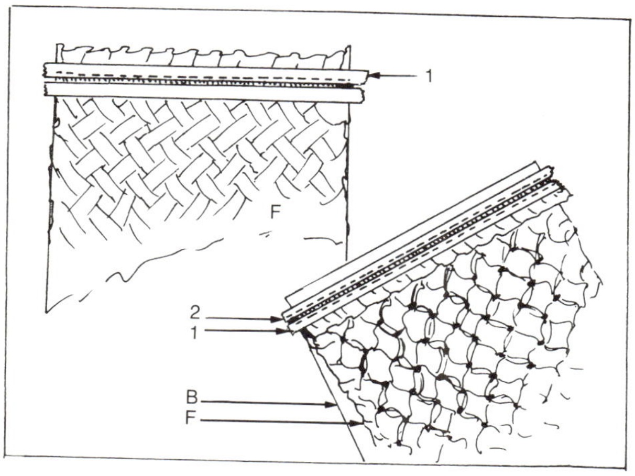

Fig. 2

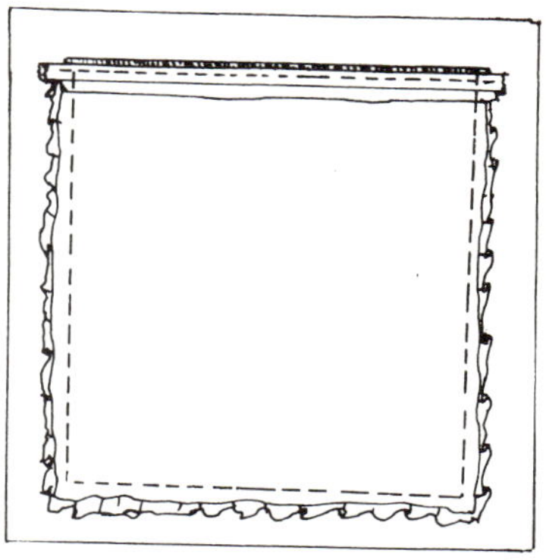

Fig. 3

Satin cushions

These beautiful cushion-covers show just how effective lattice smocking on satin can be. The covers measure 30 cm x 30 cm and have 20 cm x 20 cm smocked panels on the front. The pleats can be either broad or narrow and the cushions can be decorated further with lace or satin ribbon. They are ideal for the bedroom or as a special gift. Small flat potpourri bags can also be stitched to the cushions inside the covers.

MATERIALS
(for cover with 20 mm pleats)

1 m satin, 112 cm wide
110 cm lace or 220 cm satin ribbon, for decoration
30 cm x 30 cm cushion

Satin is often cut skew in the shop, so make sure a thread is pulled before the satin is cut.

METHOD

Follow Fig. 4 for the layout and cutting of the pattern pieces. Mark 40 mm spaced dots on the back of the 66 cm x 66 cm piece of fabric. Mark 15 dots in the first row and 14 rows of dots. Leave a 30 mm strip unmarked right round. Smock seven rows of basic lattice stitch.

Neatly fold the pleats around the edges of the smocked panel and pin or tack (see Fig. 1 of the previous cushion-cover). Strips of lace or double strips of ribbon can be stitched to side panels B and C as decoration. Using 15 mm seams throughout, stitch side panels B to two sides of smocked panel A (Fig. 5). Lightly press the seams to the inside and, making sure the smocked centre panel will measure 20 cm x 20 cm, stitch side panels C to the other two sides of smocked panel A (Fig. 6).

Stitch the three pieces E together to form the frill and lightly press in half lengthways with the right side out. Gather the frill at the open side until it measures 120 cm. Stitch a 10 mm hem along one of the sides of each piece D. Tack the frill to the front of the cover and pin it down at the corners (Fig. 7). Tack pieces D with the right sides down on top of the frill. The two seamed sides will overlap in the centre. Make sure the cover will be 30 cm x 30 cm and stitch a 15 mm seam right round, taking care not to catch the rest of the frill. Cut the seam edges even if necessary and finish off, using overcast or zigzag stitches. Turn the right side out through the back opening and lightly press the edges if necessary. Insert the cushion.

Cover with 10 mm pleats

For this cover 120 cm satin, 112 cm wide, will be required. The centre panel A should now measure 84 cm x 84 cm. Follow Fig. 8 for the layout of the pattern pieces. Mark 20 mm spaced dots. Mark 21 dots in the first row and 20 rows of dots. Smock 10 rows of basic lattice stitch. The making of the cover is the same as for the cushion-cover with wide pleats.

Variations: The covers can be made from velvet or corduroy. The frill can then be left out or replaced with piping. A zip can be stitched to the back.

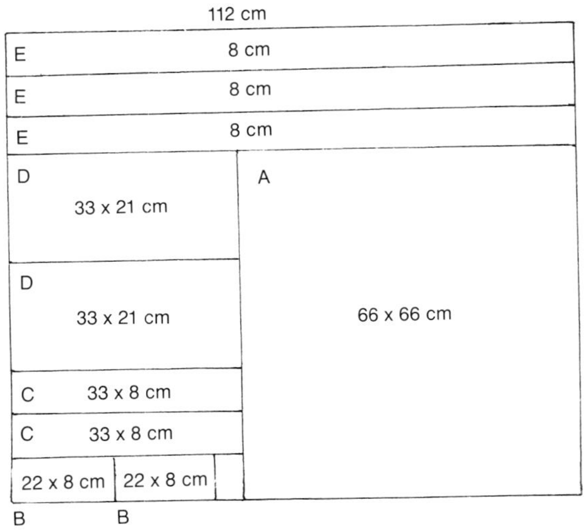

Fig. 4

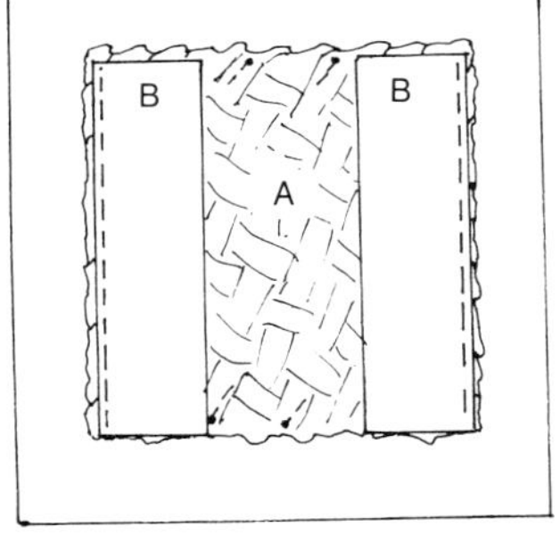

Fig. 5

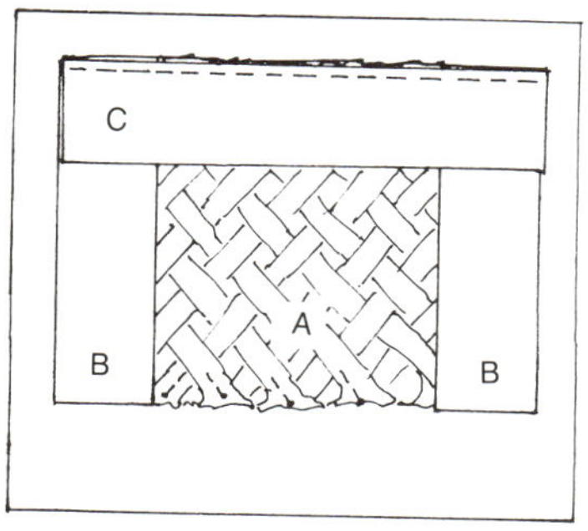

Fig. 6

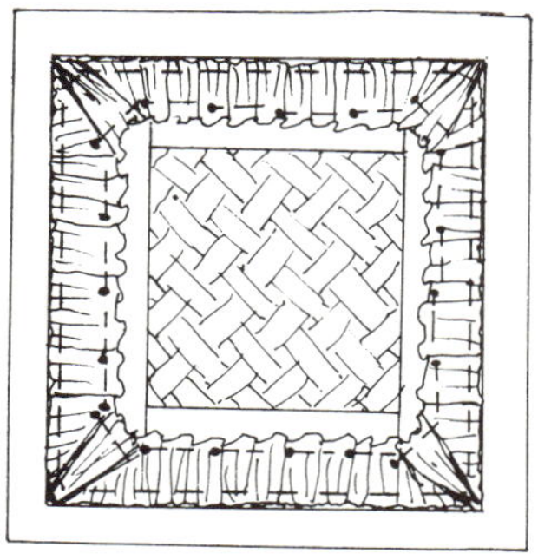

Fig. 7

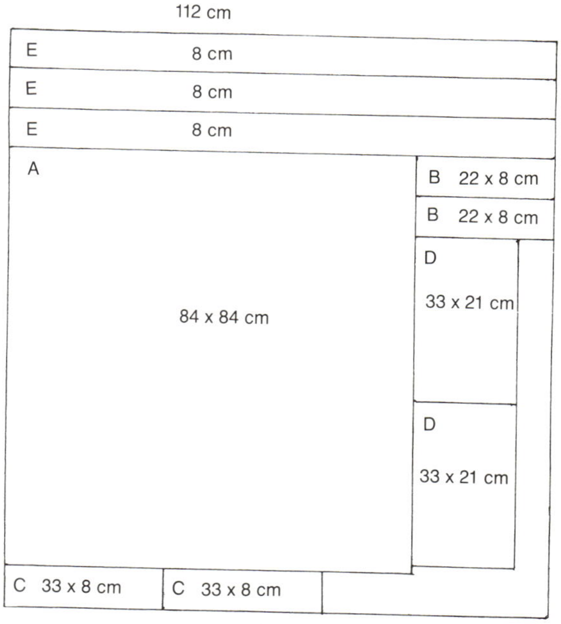

Fig. 8

Satin clutch bag

This beautiful bag was made from a square piece of smocked satin that was finished off with binding and then folded and stitched. The bag is 24 cm long. It can also be made from velvet or taffeta.

MATERIALS

90 cm x 60 cm satin (This quantity should be enough for the lining as well, if desired.)
30 cm x 24 cm black satin for the lining
One button to cover

METHOD

Cut a 60 cm x 54 cm piece of satin. Mark 20 mm spaced dots on the back. Mark 27 dots in the first row and 25 rows of dots. Smock 13 rows of basic lattice stitch across the width. Neatly fold the pleats around the edges and pin or tack (see Fig. 1 of the first cushion-cover). Cut the smocking to measure 30 cm x 24 cm.

Cut the 30 cm x 24 cm black satin and pin to the smocking with the right sides out. Cut two 32 cm x 5,5 cm and two 24 cm x 5,5 cm pieces of satin for the binding of the smocked section. First stitch the two shorter pieces to the shorter sides of the smocked section together with the lining. The right side should face the front of the smocking and the seams should be 12,5 mm. Lightly press the seams to the outside. Fold back a 12,5 mm strip. Then fold a 15 mm strip down and sew by hand along the line where it was stitched (Fig. 9). Stitch the two longer pieces to the two other sides of the smocked panel. A 7,5 mm strip will hang over on either side. Fold the two ends of this strip in and then fold over the strip itself and stitch in the same way as the two previous sides (Fig. 10). Sew the two ends by hand.

Cut a 9 cm x 4 cm piece of satin for the loop. Fold in half lengthways and stitch 7 mm from the folded edge (Fig. 11a). Stitch a second row just outside the first and cut the edge 5 mm from the stitching. Carefully turn the right side out and sew the loop to the inside of the bag in the centre of one shorter piece of binding (Fig. 11b). Fold over 11 cm of the bag and stitch or sew by hand along the inner edge of the binding (Fig. 12a). Fold over the bag 6,5 cm from the side with the loop. Cover the button with satin and sew onto the bag at the loose end of the loop (Fig. 12b).

Variations: The bag can be made with an extra inner pocket closed with a zip. Cut a 24 cm x 14 cm piece of black satin. First stitch one side of a 22 cm long zip to this piece of satin and then stitch the other side to the front of the lining (Fig. 13a). Fold the loose piece down, fold a small seam at the lower end and stitch to the lining (Fig. 13b). Now pin the lining to the smocked panel.

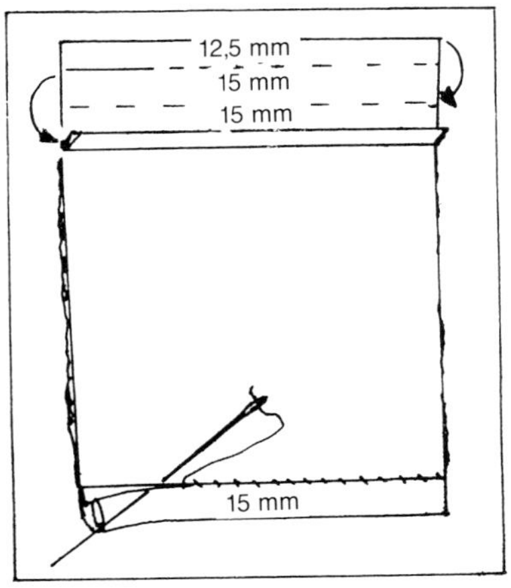

Fig. 9

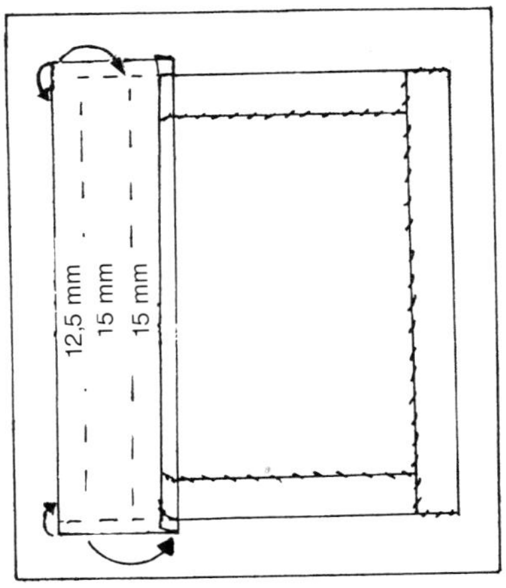

Fig. 10

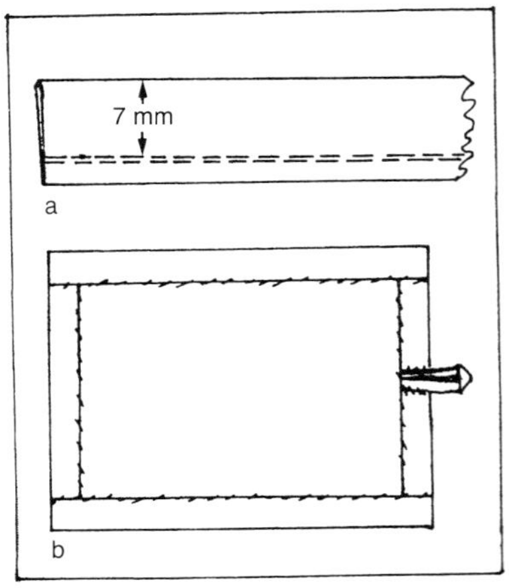

Fig. 11

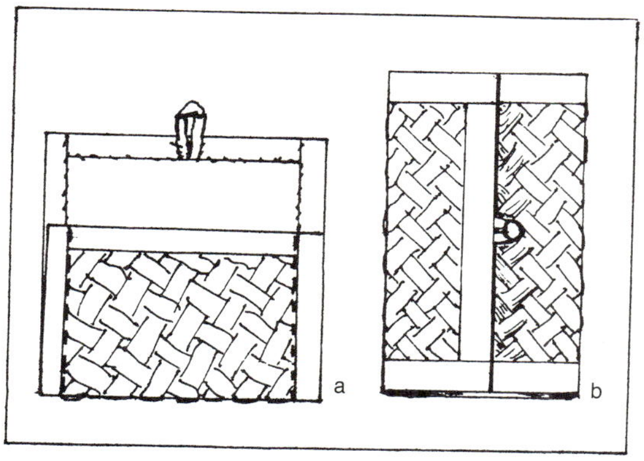

Fig. 12

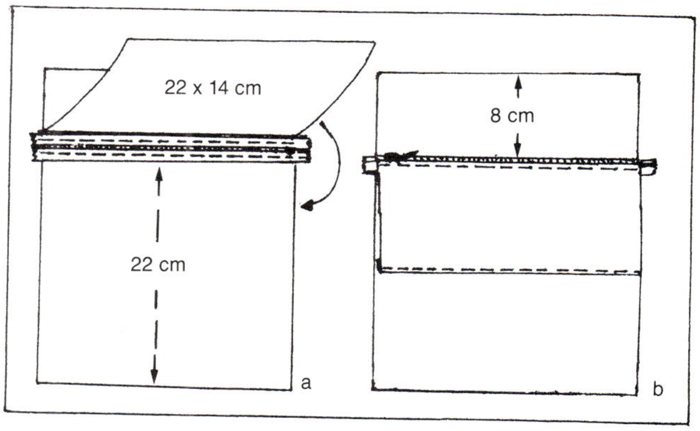

Fig. 13

Belts

Belts like these can transform simple dresses into smart outfits. The white satin belt is 6 cm wide and was smocked in basic lattice stitch. The brown velvet belt is 8 cm wide and was smocked in lattice stitch with rows left open in between. The belts can also be made to match the evening bags.

Satin belt

MATERIALS

30 cm satin or 40 cm velvet, 90 cm wide
A piece of leftover fabric for the lining
Two buttons to cover or a decorative buckle

The lining can be strengthened with iron-on interfacing if it is not stiff enough.

METHOD

Cut the satin twice the length of the finished belt and 15 cm wide (see p. 5 how fabric is joined). Mark the entire back of the fabric with 20 mm spaced dots. Smock rows of basic lattice stitch across the width of the fabric. Neatly fold the pleats around the edges of the smocking and pin or tack (Fig. 1 on p. 9). Cut two 70 mm x 40 mm pieces of satin for the two loops. Fold in half lengthways and stitch 7 mm from the folded edge. Stitch a second row along the first and cut the edge 5 mm from the stitching (see Fig. 11a of the satin clutch bag). Carefully turn the right sides out.

Cut the lining 70 mm wide and 30 mm longer than the finished belt. Strengthen with iron-on interfacing if necessary. Stitch the lining lengthways to one side of the smocked section with the right side facing the front of the belt (Fig. 14a). Fold the lining back and sew the other side and ends of the lining by hand (Fig. 14b). The long sides of the lining should be 5 mm narrower than the belt. The two loops are sewn in at one end of the belt. Cover the two buttons with satin and sew them to the other end of the belt. Some of the other variations of lattice smocking can also be used for this belt.

Velvet belt

MATERIALS
(see materials for satin belt)

METHOD

Cut two 20 cm strips of velvet and stitch together. Make sure the nap of the fabric runs in the same direction on both sides of the join. Mark the entire piece with 20 mm spaced dots. Smock four rows of ordinary lattice stitch across the width at the ends of the belt. Leave every third row open in the centre section of the belt. Make sure the belt is long enough for the ends to overlap by at least 12 cm. This belt is finished off with black leather piping.

Cut the lining 10 cm wide and 20 mm longer than the belt. Tack the right side of the lining to the right side of the smocked panel and stitch a 10 mm seam along the two long sides and one end. If piping is used, it should be stitched on at the same time. Turn the right side out and sew the open end by hand. If the buckle is used, it should be sewn to one end, together with press studs at the back. If preferred, this belt can be finished off in the same way as the previous belt.

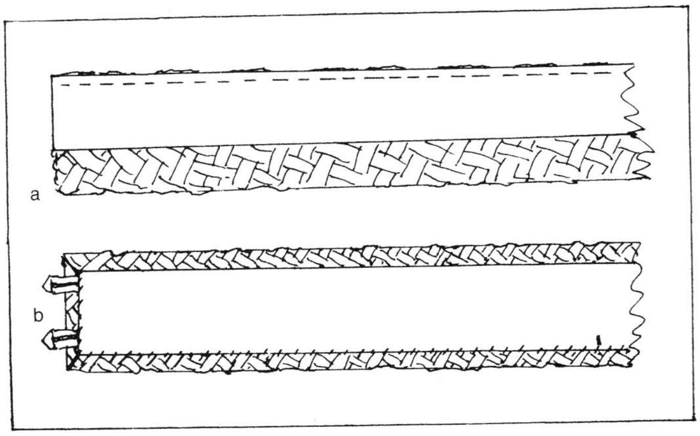

Fig. 14

Round velvet cushions

These cushions are truly very special and will always evoke admiration. The dark blue cushion has two rows of smocking and the light blue one has three. The smocking therefore does not take much time. Leftover pieces of soft upholstery fabric were used for these cushions.

Light blue cushion

MATERIALS
(for cushion 32 cm in diameter and 10 cm wide)

Velvet or soft upholstery fabric, 75 cm long and 120 cm wide or 60 cm long and 150 cm wide
Strong matching sewing thread
A foam cushion, 30 cm in diameter and 10 cm thick
Two buttons to cover, 30 mm in diameter

Thinner pieces of foam can be glued on top of one another and a circle can be cut from this for the cushion.

METHOD

Cutting: A 114 cm x 53 cm piece of fabric is needed for the smocking. If the fabric is 150 cm wide, the piece should be cut across the fabric. It then does not have to be joined. If the fabric is 120 cm wide, two 75 cm x 53 cm pieces should be cut out next to one another and then stitched together. The nap of the two pieces should run in the same direction on both sides of the join. Cut the seam edges to 15 mm and finish off together, using overcast or zigzag stitches. Enough leftover fabric will remain on one side of both widths of fabric to cover the buttons.
Marking and smocking: Fig. 15 shows how the fabric is marked. Mark 2,5 cm-spaced dots lengthways along the centre of the fabric. Mark nine dots in the first row and 57 rows of dots. Leave a 16 cm unmarked strip on both sides. Stitch the ends of the strip together so that the first row of dots lies exactly on top of the last row. Cut the seam edges to 15 mm and finish off together, using overcast or zigzag stitches. Smock three rows of basic lattice stitch right round, leaving half a row between the smocked rows. Fold the seam to one side at the join and smock over it.

Pull the smocked fabric over the cushion so that the smocked strip fits neatly over the edge of the cushion. Fold each pleat neatly to the centre on one side of the cushion and, using a strong thread, tack through the end of each pleat (Fig. 16). Make sure the pleats meet in the centre of the cushion without overlapping. If they do overlap, cut off some of the fabric. Gather the tacking thread tightly and firmly sew the ends together at the centre of the cushion. Fold the pleats on the other side of the cushion in the same way and sew the ends together. Cover the two buttons with fabric. Using very strong thread or thin string, thread through the ring of one button, pull the ends through the centre of the cushion with a long upholstery needle and thread through the ring of the other button on the other side of the cushion (Fig. 17). The buttons should draw the cushion slightly inward at the centre.

Dark blue cushion

MATERIALS
(for cushion 32 cm in diameter and 8 cm wide)

Velvet or soft upholstery fabric, 70 cm long and 120 cm wide or 50 cm long and 150 cm wide
Strong matching sewing thread
A foam cushion, 30 cm in diameter and 8 cm thick
Two buttons to cover, 30 mm in diameter

METHOD

Cutting: A piece of fabric 134 cm x 48,5 cm is needed for the smocking. If the fabric is 150 cm wide, the piece can be cut across the width of the fabric. If the fabric is 120 cm wide, two pieces, each 70 cm x 48,5 cm, should be cut out next to one another and then joined in the same way as for the light blue cushion.
Marking and smocking: Mark the fabric in the same way as the previous cushion but this time mark six dots in the first row and 53 rows of dots. Mark 2,5 mm spaced dots, leaving an 18 cm unmarked strip on both sides. Stitch the two sides together so that the first row of dots lies exactly on top of the last row. Cut the seam edges to 15 mm and finish off together. Smock two rows of basic lattice stitch right round, leaving half a row between the smocked rows.

Make the cushion in the same way as the previous cushion.

Variations: The cushions can be smocked in heavy satin. The patterns can be adapted for smaller or larger cushions but it may then be necessary to smock the fabric first before the last seam is stitched. Smock the fabric to just before the seam, pull the fabric over the foam cushion to obtain the right length for the circumference and then stitch the seam. Then smock the piece across the seam.

Fig. 16

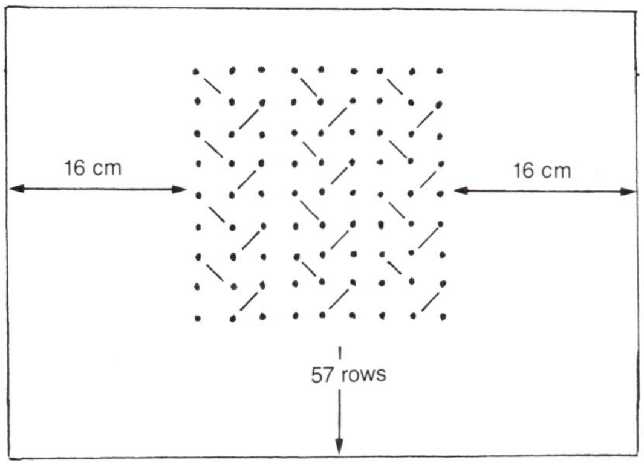

Fig. 15

Fig. 17

Coat-hanger covers

These lattice-smocked coat-hangers make beautiful gifts and can be made from small pieces of leftover satin or taffeta. The same pattern was used for these two covers but one was smocked in basic lattice stitch and the other in reverse basic lattice stitch.

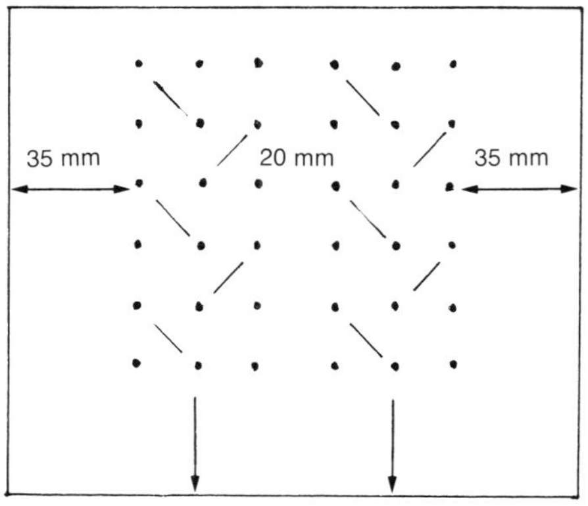

Fig. 18

MATERIALS
(for one hanger)

70 cm x 15 cm taffeta or satin
45 cm long wooden coat-hanger
50 cm matching satin ribbon, 15 mm wide
Strips of thin foam rubber to cover the hanger

METHOD

Marking and smocking: Fig. 18 shows how the dots are marked. Mark 15 mm spaced dots with a 20 mm space between the two rows. Leave a 35 mm unmarked strip on both sides. For the one hanger, the dots were marked on the back of the fabric and two rows of basic lattice stitch were smocked over the entire length. For the other hanger, the dots were marked on the front and two rows of reverse basic lattice stitch were smocked.

The coat-hanger should be covered to give it a soft surface. Do this by cutting strips of foam, twisting them around the hanger and sewing down the ends. The hanger can also be covered with strips of soft fabric or even strips of old tights. Fold the smocked cover in half and cut a small hole in the centre for the wire hook. The hole can be finished off with small buttonhole stitches if necessary. Neatly fold the pleats down on the sides of the smocking and tack (Fig. 1 on p. 9). Fold the cover over the hanger and sew together at the bottom by hand. Fig. 19 shows how the pleats are folded down and one side is sewed over the other. If the part folded underneath is too long, cut off some of the fabric.

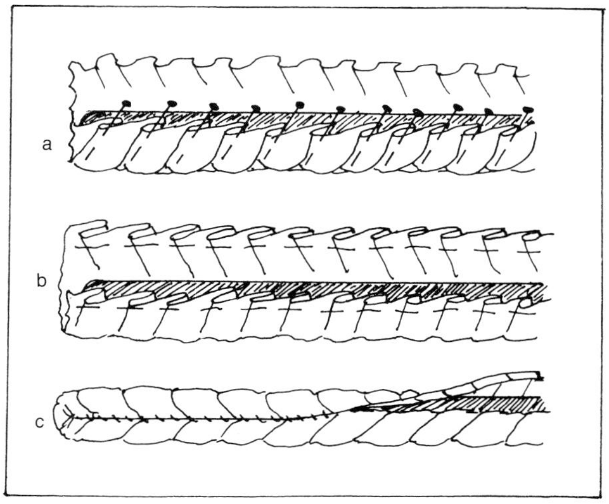

Fig. 19

Cut 25 cm of ribbon, fold 10 mm in at the ends and fold the ribbon in half lengthways with the right side out. Using matching pearl cotton thread or embroidery yarn, tack small stitches along the side of the ribbon (Fig. 20a). Cover the wire hook with the ribbon and, with the tacking on the outside of the hook, gather the tacking thread tightly. Sew the end to the cover (Fig. 20b). Tie a bow from the remaining 25 cm of ribbon and sew to the bottom of the covered wire hook.

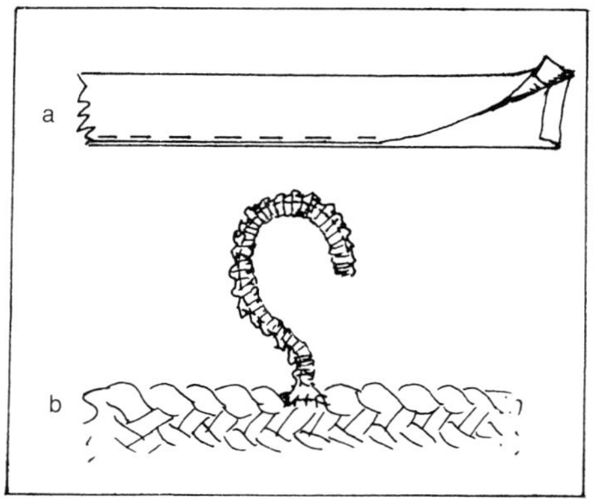

Fig. 20

Round satin bag

This is a lovely example of how reverse basic lattice smocking can be used. Small beads were incorporated to give a touch of elegance to the bag.

MATERIALS

85 cm x 37 cm satin or taffeta
65 cm x 20 cm black satin for the lining
About 125 small glass or pearl beads
60 cm matching cord

METHOD

Cutting and smocking: Cut a 64 cm x 37 cm piece of fabric for the outside of the bag. Fold back a 5 cm strip and press lightly. Fig. 21 shows how the dots are marked on the front of the fabric. Start the first row 45 mm from the folded edge. Mark 20 mm spaced dots and 13 horizontal rows of dots. Smock five strips of two rows each, leaving one row between the strips. Either do not mark the dots of these open rows or mark them with air-soluble ink. Fold open the folded strip and stitch the two shorter sides together with a 15 mm seam. Leave a 10 mm opening in this seam 11 cm from the top or 6 cm from the folded edge. Press open the seam and finish off the seam edge. Fold back the folded edge and smock double rows in reverse basic lattice stitch (Fig. 22). Catch the folded edge at the back with the first stitch of every row. Incorporate the beads with every second stitch. Neatly fold down the pleats at the bottom edge of the smocking and tack or pin. Do the same for the pleats at the folded edge and tack or pin. The circumference at the folded edge should be 45 cm after the pleats have been folded.

Cut a 17 cm diameter circle from the fabric and stitch it with a 10 mm seam to the lower edge of the smocked piece to form the bottom of the bag. Cut the seams edges even and finish off. Cut a 48 cm x 20 cm piece of lining and stitch the two shorter sides together with a 15 mm seam. Press open the seam and finish off. Cut a 17 cm diameter circle from the lining fabric and stitch to one side of the lining with a 15 mm seam. Stitch a 15 mm hem at the other opening. Leave a 10 mm opening in this hem at the seam to thread the cord. Turn the wrong side of the lining out, thread the cord and place the lining inside the bag (Fig. 23a). The upper edge of the lining should be 45 mm from the folded edge of the bag and the seams of the bag and lining together. Bring out the ends of the cord through the opening in the seam of the bag. Knot the ends of the cord or tie them neatly. Sew the upper edge of the lining by hand to the inside of the folded edge of the bag (45 mm from the top) (Fig. 23b). Make sure not to catch the cord or that the stitches do not show on the front of the bag.

Variations: This round evening bag can be made from soft velvet and the beads can be omitted. The upper edge of the satin bag can be decorated further with beads.

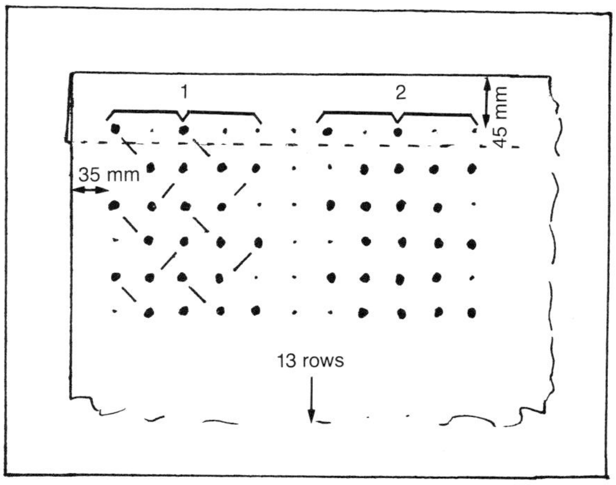

Fig. 21

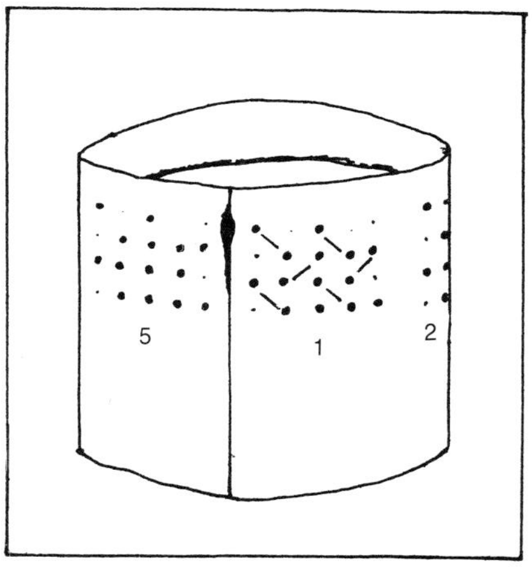

Fig. 22

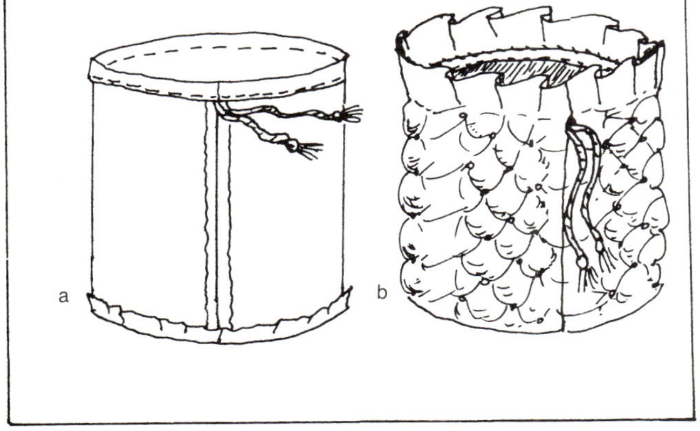

Fig. 23

Potpourri bags

These attractive and fragrant grosgrain bags can be hung in the linen or clothes cupboard or placed among underwear. They can also be displayed in the bedroom with cushions. Bags like these, filled with homemade potpourri, make very special and appreciated gifts.

Lilac bag

This bag measures 15 cm x 15 cm and is filled with fragrant lavender potpourri. It was smocked with rows on alternate sides.

MATERIALS

50 cm x 30 cm grosgrain silk or taffeta
50 cm matching satin ribbon, 15 mm wide
125 cm cotton lace
Leftover cotton fabric for the inner bag
A handful of fragrant lavender or other potpourri

METHOD

Marking and smocking: Cut a 30 cm x 30 cm piece of fabric. Fig. 24 shows how the dots are marked. Mark and smock rows 1, 3 and 5 on the front and mark and smock rows 2 and 4 on the back. Mark 15 mm spaced dots, leaving 20 mm between the rows. There should be 17 horizontal rows of dots. Follow the method for smocking rows on alternate sides and smock five rows in alternate directions. Cut a 17 cm x 17 cm square for the back of the bag. Gather the lace or pleat it around the outer edge on the front of the square for the back (Fig. 25). Tack and, with the right sides together, place on the smocked square. Stitch a 10 mm seam right round, leaving a 9 cm opening on one side. Cut the seams even and edge. Turn the right side out through the opening. Make a 14 cm x 14 cm inner bag from soft cotton fabric, fill with the potpourri and stitch closed. Place the inner bag inside the smocked one and oversew the opening by hand. Stitch a 20 cm ribbon loop to the bag and decorate further with a bow tied from the leftover ribbon.

Heart-shaped bag

This 18 cm wide bag is filled with rose potpourri. It was smocked with reverse basic lattice stitch.

MATERIALS

55 cm x 30 cm grosgrain silk or taffeta
1 m matching cotton lace
50 cm matching satin ribbon, 15 mm wide
Leftover cotton fabric for the inner bag
A handful of fragrant rose or other potpourri

METHOD

Marking and smocking: Cut a 32 cm x 30 cm piece of fabric and mark the dots on the front of the fabric as shown in Fig. 26. Mark 15 mm spaced dots and 20 horizontal rows of dots. Smock every second row down. Do not mark the dots for the rows in between. Smock five rows of reverse basic lattice stitch. Trace the heart-shaped pattern on p. 32 and cut one heart from the fabric for the back. Pleat the lace around the edge on the right side of the back and tack as for the previous bag (Fig. 25). Place the back, with the right sides together, on the smocked panel and tack as for the previous bag. The middle row should be in the centre of the heart. It is not necessary to cut a heart from the smocking first. Stitch a 10 mm seam round the heart, leaving a 10 cm opening on one side. Cut the smocked section away along the seam edge. Cut into the seam as far as the stitching at the V of the heart and finish off. Turn the right side out through the opening. Cut two hearts from the cotton and stitch a 15 mm seam right round, leaving an 8 cm opening on one side. Cut into the seam as far as the stitching at the V of the heart. Turn the right side out, fill with the potpourri and stitch closed. Place the inner bag inside the smocked heart and oversew the opening by hand.

Variations: The bags can be cut into various shapes and sizes and any of the lattice stitch variations can be used for the smocking. The bags can be decorated with a frill from the same fabric instead of lace. Beads can be incorporated with the reverse basic lattice smocking.

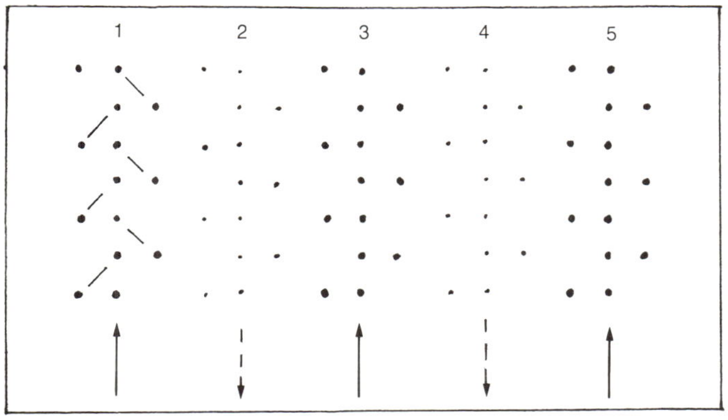

Fig. 24

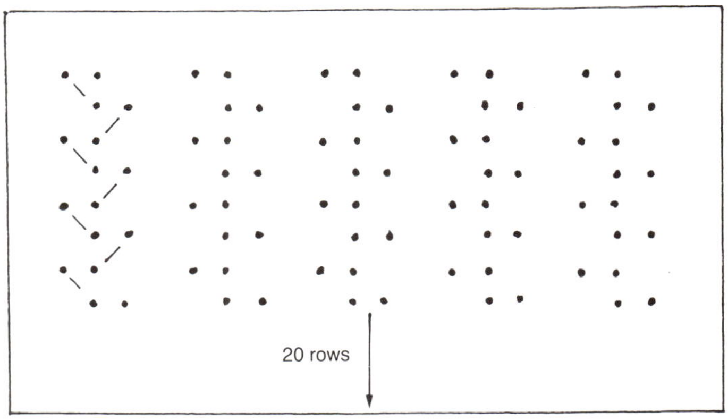

Fig. 26

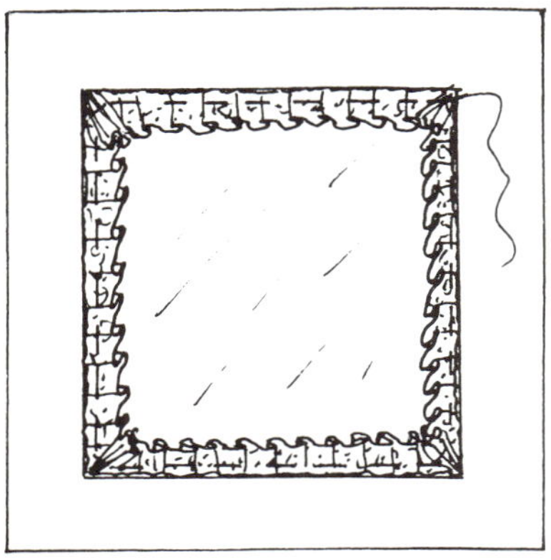

Fig. 25

Toilet set

These cream covers for a toilet seat and toilet-paper will add femininity and a touch of old-fashioned grace to any bathroom or toilet. Taffeta was used for this set but satin or even velvet can also be used.

MATERIALS FOR THE SET

125 cm taffeta, 112 cm wide
2 m matching satin ribbon, 8 cm wide
40 cm matching satin ribbon, 15 mm wide (or 40 cm bias binding)
60 cm cotton lace about 3 cm wide with holes for threading
38 cm x 35 cm thin batting

The lining (piece B) and the fastening strip (piece D) for the seat cover can also be made from unbleached cotton or other fabric.

Cover for toilet seat lid

METHOD

This cover measures 38 x 33 cm but the measurements can easily be adapted for toilets of different sizes. Trace the outline of the toilet lid onto a piece of paper. Mark the back and front points on the pattern. Add a 15 mm seam right round and cut out the pattern. Use this pattern to cut out piece B. See Fig. 27 on how to cut out the pieces for the set.

Fig. 30 shows how the dots are marked on piece A. Mark row 4 in the centre of the fabric. Mark and smock rows 1, 3, 5 and 7 on the back of the fabric. Mark rows 2, 4 and 6 on the front and smock with reverse basic lattice stitch. Follow the method for rows on alternate sides on p. 8 and smock the entire piece. Neatly fold the pleats on the sides and pin. Place the pattern for the lid on this smocked piece and cut out. The middle row should be in the centre of the cut piece. Mark the back point. Neatly fold the pleats around this piece and tack. Stitch pieces C together for the frill. Fold a 15 mm strip in at both ends. Press open the joining seam and then press the piece in half lengthways. The right side should be out. Gather or pleat the frill until it is 119 cm long (the circumference of the lid) and tack on top of the smocked piece. The ends of the frill should just meet in the centre at the back of the smocked piece.

Cut off the 15 mm seam of the pattern for the toilet lid and then use this pattern to cut the batting for the lid. Stitch a narrow hem on both short sides of piece D. Stitch a 15 mm hem along one long side. Place the layers for the lid on top of one another: first the lining (piece B) with the right side down; then the batting; then smocked piece A with the right side up and the frill pinned to it; and then fastening strip D with the wrong side up and the hem to the inside (Fig. 29). The ends of fastening strip D should come to about 7 cm from the centre on the back of the smocked piece. Make sure the back points of all the layers are on top of one another. Tack the layers and stitch a 15 mm seam right round. Cut the seam edges even if necessary and finish off. Fold the fastening strip back and lightly press down if necessary. Thread 120 cm of the narrow ribbon through the hem of the fastening strip. Cover the lid with the cover, gather the ribbon and tie a bow on the inside of the lid.

Cover for toilet-roll

METHOD

See Fig. 28 on how to mark the dots on piece E. Leave a 6 cm unmarked strip at the top. Stitch the short sides of piece E together with a 10 mm seam after the dots have been marked. Make sure the first row of vertical dots is exactly on the last row. Press the seam open. The seam should be in the middle of one row. The smocking is the same as for the toilet lid cover. Smock rows 2, 4, 6, etc., on the back, turn over and smock the rows in between – 1, 3, 5, etc. – on the front. Neatly fold the pleats at the bottom of the smocking and tack or pin. Stitch the short sides of strip F together for the frill. Press the seam open and then press the strip in half lengthways with the right side out. Gather the frill or pleat it to measure 38 cm. Tack it on the front at the bottom of the smocked circle. Tack or pin the wide ribbon (or bias binding) with the right side down on top (Fig. 31). Where the ends of the ribbon overlap, fold the lower end back 10 mm. This stitches more easily if the right side (RS) of the smocked cylinder is turned out. Stitch a 15 mm seam all along the edge of the ribbon. Turn the cylinder with the right side out again. Fold the ribbon to the inside and stitch along the free edge of the ribbon (Fig. 32). This stitching shows on the front of the smocking but is later covered with the lace.

Sew the two ends of the lace together. Thread about

56 cm of the ribbon through the lace, pull it over the smocked cover and gather the ribbon. Spread out the pleats in the lace evenly. The lace should cover the stitching at the bottom of the cover. Tie a bow with the ends of the ribbon. Pull the cover over a roll of toilet-paper and fold the pleats at the top of the cover to meet neatly in the centre. Sew together and cover the stitching with a small bow tied from the leftover ribbon. Small silk flowers can also be stitched on the cover as decoration.

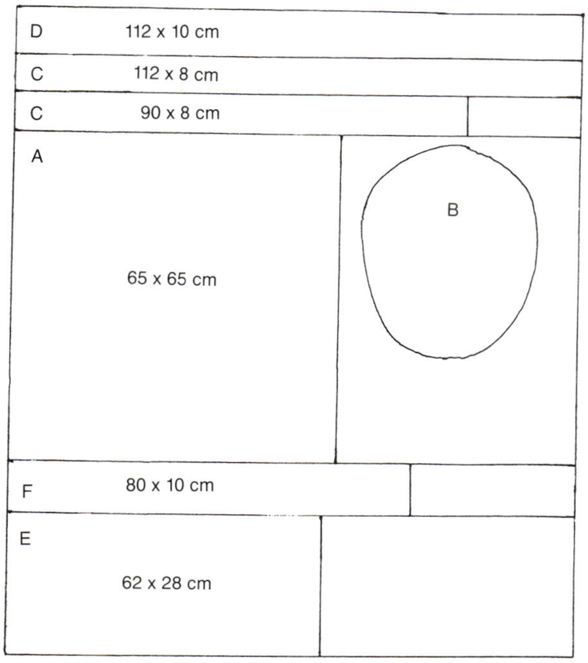

Fig. 27

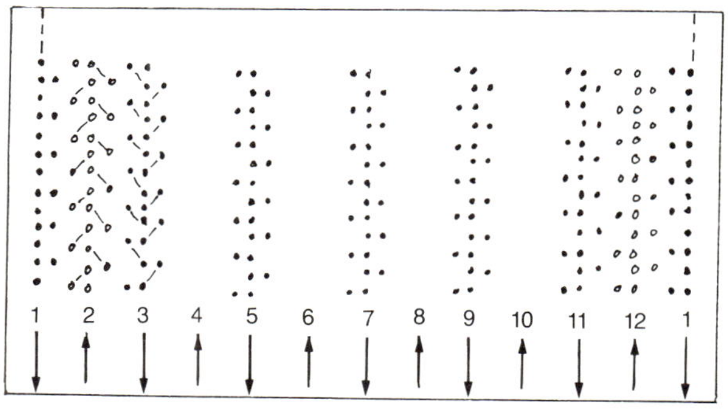

Fig. 30

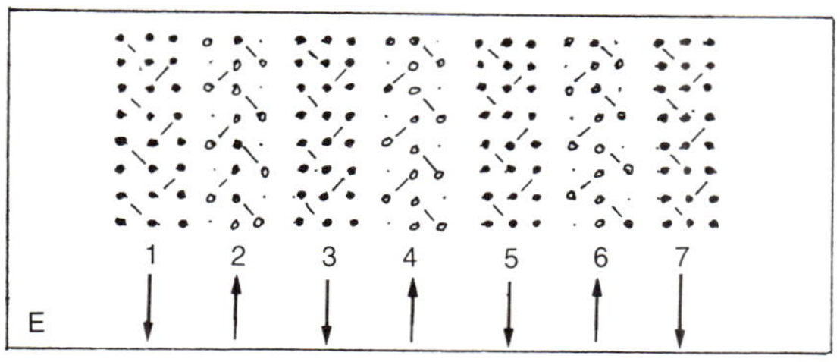

Fig. 28

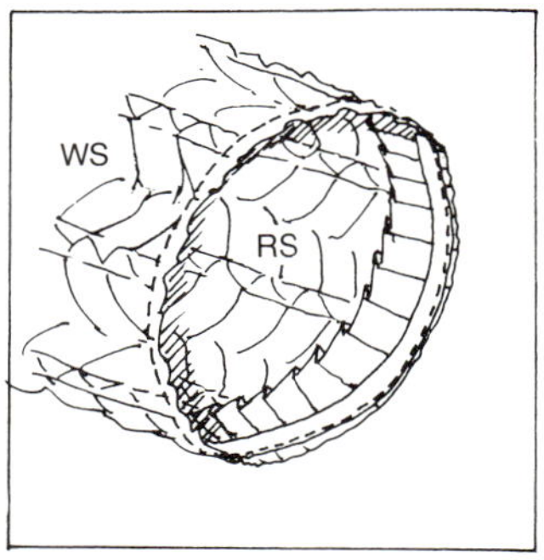

Fig. 31

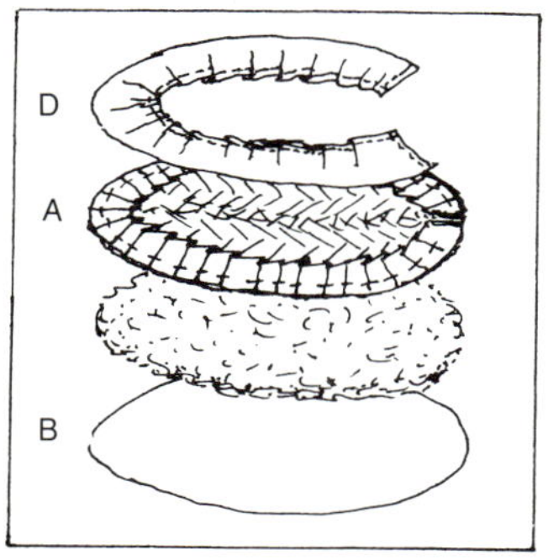

Fig. 29

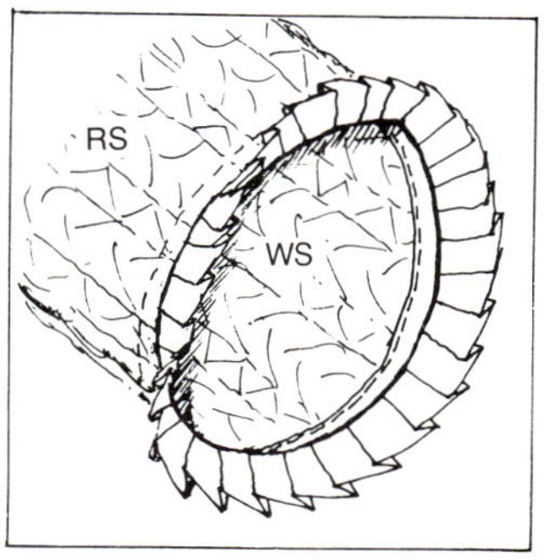

Fig. 32

Satin waistcoat

This satin waistcoat was smocked in reverse basic lattice stitch and is really something special. Two half open rows and a central strip with rows on alternate sides were smocked on the back. The waistcoat can also form part of a bridal gown: it can be made from white satin decorated with small pearls and worn over a simple white long-sleeved dress.

MATERIALS

120 cm satin, 150 cm wide
90 cm lining, 112 cm wide

These quantities should be enough for a waistcoat up to size 14. Any simple waistcoat pattern without darts can be used. The shoulder and underarm seams should not be cut off. Any seams around the outer edges and armholes should be cut off.

METHOD

Marking and smocking: For the front panels, a piece of satin twice the width and twice the length of the pattern is required. Mark 20 mm spaced dots on the front of the fabric. Smock the entire piece with reverse basic lattice stitch. If the pattern is placed on the smocking every now and then, the parts to be cut away around the neck and armhole can be left unsmocked. The smocking should extend at least 20 mm over the pattern right round. Pin the pattern to the smocking and stitch right round, using zigzag stitches (Fig. 33). Cut off the fabric just outside the stitching. For the back panel, the fabric should measure double the length and about double the width of the pattern. See Fig. 34 on how to mark and smock the back panel. Mark 20 mm spaced dots. Do not mark the dots that are not to be smocked. Edge the smocked back panel, using zigzag stitches as for the front panel and cut off the fabric just outside the stitching.

Use the same pattern pieces to cut the lining. Stitch the shoulder and underarm seams of the smocked section and the lining. Lightly press the seams open. Tack or pin the lining to the smocking with the wrong sides together. Use the leftover satin to cut 5 cm wide strips on the bias for piping. Measure the outer edges of the waistcoat and the armholes and cut the bias binding so that there are as few joins as possible. The front of the bias binding should be on the front of the smocking. Try to stitch the bias binding so that the joins are inconspicuous. Stitch the bias binding with a 10 mm seam around the outer edges of the waistcoat and the armholes. Fold the bias binding to the inside, fold a 10 mm seam to the inside and sew by hand. The piping should be 15 mm wide. Lightly press the piping if necessary.

Variations: Any of the lattice stitch variations can be used. Small beads or pearls can be incorporated in the joining stitches. A long-sleeved jacket can be cut and made from smocking in the same way; a simple pattern without darts should be used for this.

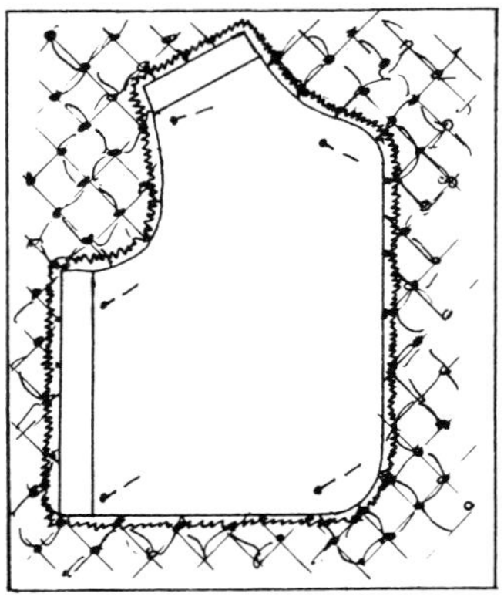

Fig. 33

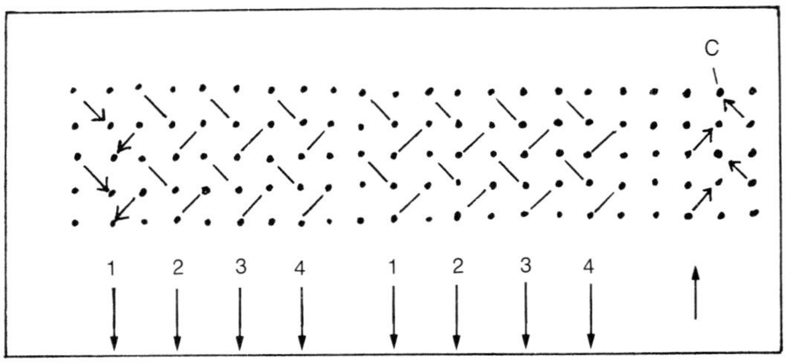

Fig. 34

C = centre back

Photo frames

These attractive frames can be made very quickly and will be greatly appreciated as gifts. They were made from taffeta and measure 21 cm x 15 cm. The pattern for the dark blue frame can easily be adapted for larger frames.

Dark blue frame

MATERIALS

50 cm taffeta or some leftover taffeta
Thick cardboard
Sharp paper knife
Adhesive
Short pieces of matching satin ribbon
A 18 cm x 12 cm piece of glass (optional)
Photo

METHOD

Cut a 45 cm x 30 cm piece of taffeta and mark 20 mm spaced dots on the back. Mark 19 dots in the first row and 12 rows of dots. Smock the entire piece with basic lattice stitch.

Cut two 21 cm x 15 cm pieces and one 15 cm x 8 cm piece of cardboard. Cut a 18 cm x 18 cm piece of taffeta. Fold in half and stitch a 1 cm seam on two sides (Fig. 35a). Turn out and insert the smaller piece of cardboard to form the stand. Fold 1 cm of fabric to the inside at the opening. Cut a 29 cm x 21 cm piece of taffeta and sew the top of the covered stand to the right side of this piece (Fig. 35b). Glue where the stand was stitched and cover one of the bigger pieces of cardboard with the fabric. Glue the edges of the fabric to the back (Fig. 36a). This covered board will form the back of the frame.

Cut a 13 cm x 9 cm oval opening in the other big piece of cardboard. Use an oval box or something similar to obtain the oval shape. Cover this piece of cardboard with the smocking and glue the edges of the fabric (Fig. 36b). Use clothes-pegs to keep the fabric in place until the glue has dried completely. Cut away the smocking over the oval opening, leaving 20 mm of fabric to be folded back. The fabric folds back more easily if the smocking stitches on the fabric that is folded back, are cut. Clip the fabric every 20 mm to just before the folded edge. Fold and glue (Fig. 37a). Glue in four separate parts, otherwise there will not be enough room for the clothes-pegs around the edges. Cut off any excess fabric. If the photo is to be covered with glass, glue it now on the back over the oval opening. Glue the photo to the inside of the back cover and then glue the back to the front. Cut a 12 cm piece of ribbon and sew the ends 40 mm from the bottom of the back of the frame and 40 mm from the bottom of the stand (Fig. 37b).

Light blue frame

MATERIALS
(see materials for dark blue frame)

METHOD

Cut a 38 cm x 30 cm piece of taffeta and mark the dots on the front as shown in Fig. 38. Follow the direction of the arrows and smock rows of basic lattice stitch. Neatly fold the pleats when glueing the smocking over the cardboard. Follow the method above to make the frame. The frame can be decorated with bows tied from matching satin ribbon.

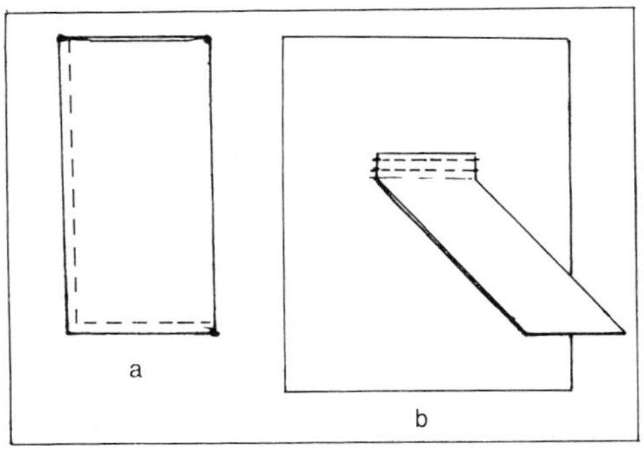

Fig. 35

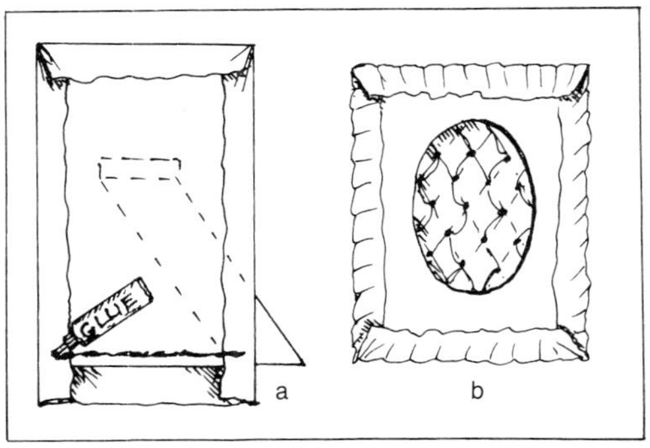

Fig. 36

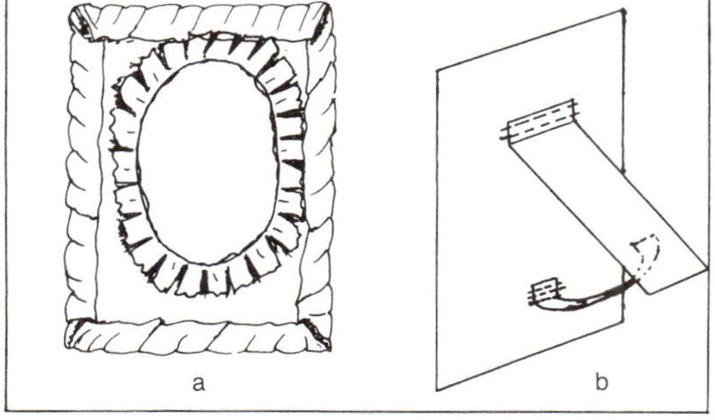

Fig. 37

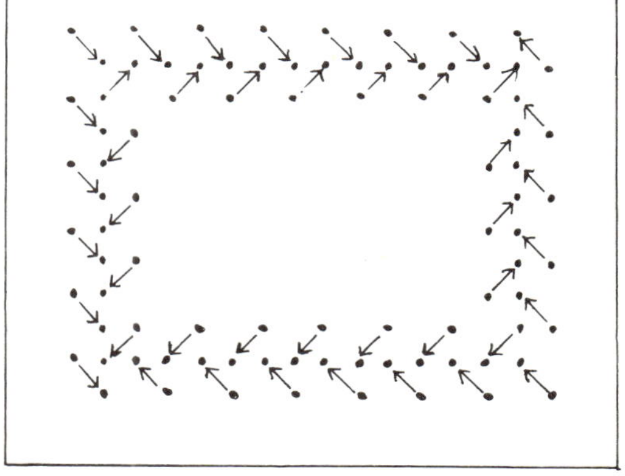

Fig. 38

Lattice smocking on garments

This section provides some ideas on other ways in which this smocking can be used.

Dress

This dress was made from crease-resistant synthetic fabric. The bodice was smocked with strips of reverse basic lattice stitch. One row was left open between the strips. Two rows of reverse basic lattice stitch were smocked on the front of the bodice in the centre. The dots are 20 mm apart and pearls were incorporated at the joining stitches. Only the bodice was lined and it was finished off with piping at the top. One side-seam has a zip. If a fuller skirt is required, no rows should be left open on the bodice.

The entire bodice of a dress can be smocked in this way. The neck and armholes should then be cut from the smocking according to the pattern.

Blouse with smocked sleeves

A fine synthetic crease-resistant knit was used for this blouse. Pieces of fabric were smocked beforehand with rows of reverse basic lattice stitch and the sleeves were then cut from these pieces. One row was left open between the smocking. The dots were spaced 20 mm apart and small matching beads were incorporated at each point that was joined. Any pattern for a blouse can be used as long as the sleeve panels are not too wide. The top of the front and back panels can also be smocked to form yokes and to provide fullness.

Tracksuit

This tracksuit top shows how effectively tracksuit fabric can be smocked. The tops of the sleeves were smocked to give the sleeves more fullness. Any other part of the tracksuit can also be cut from smocking done beforehand.

Skirt

This skirt shows how well this smocking can be used for the skirt of a bridal gown or an evening dress. The top was marked on the back with 20 mm spaced dots. All the vertical rows were smocked first, every third row was left open from the seventh row of dots and, lastly, from the 16th to the 25th row of dots, six rows were left open and two were smocked. If heavy satin is used, the pleats between the smocked rows will be more conspicuous than with softer fabric.

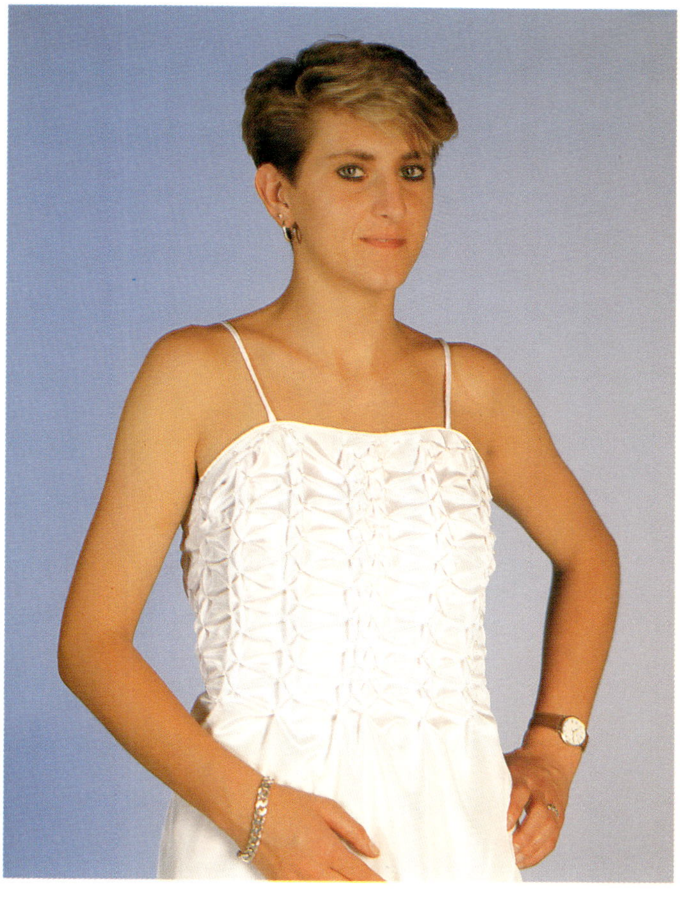

References

Canadian smocking
Thom, M. *Smocking in embroidery*, p.85-86. Batsford (1972).

Lattice smocking
Golden Hands encyclopedia of embroidery, p.124-126. Collins (1973).

Pleated smocked cushions
The complete book of knitting, crochet and embroidery, p.442-445. Cavendish (1977).

North American smocking
Smocking. Needlecrafts no. 5, p.29-31. Search Press (1979).

North American smocking
Andrew, A. *Smocking*, p.39-40. Delos (1989).

Heart pattern